THE EXTRAORDINARY LIFE OF
FREDDIE
MERCURY

Written by Michael Lee Richardson
Illustrated by Maggie Cole

EXTRAORDINARY LIVES

PUFFIN

Zanzibar, Tanzania

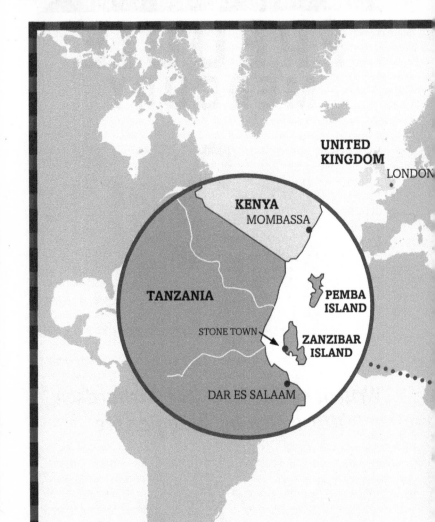

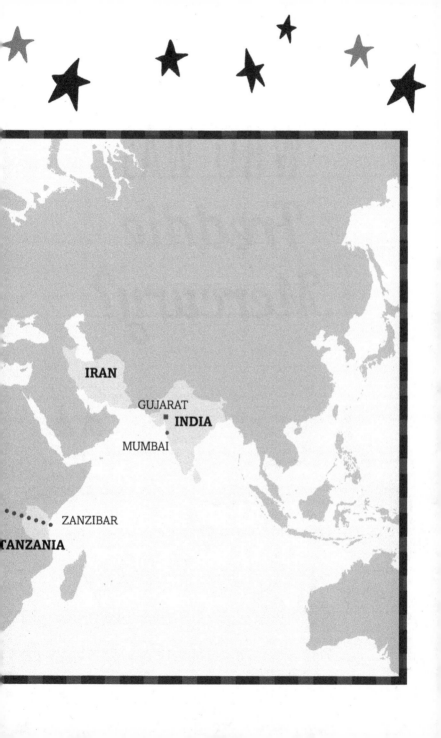

WHO WAS
Freddie
Mercury?

Freddie Mercury

was born Farrokh Bulsara in Stone Town, Zanzibar, in Tanzania, Africa, on 5 September 1946.

His parents, Bomi and Jer, were Persian, and had moved
to Zanzibar from India to find work. Bomi and Jer were
both Parsis, followers of the ZOROASTRIAN religion.
Farrokh also had a little sister, named Kashmira.

ZOROASTRIANISM is the ancient religion of Iran that is practised in some areas there, and more so in India. The founder of the religion is generally thought to be the Iranian prophet Zoroaster (also known as Zarathustra) back in the sixth century BCE, and Zoroastrianism probably influenced other major Western religions like Christianity, Islam and Judaism.

When he was eight years old Farrokh was sent to a **boarding school** near Mumbai in India, which was called Bombay at the time. Though he was **shy at first**, he soon began to make friends, and was clearly talented in art and sport. But Farrokh's biggest passion was **music**. He was always playing records around the house, and had very ECLECTIC tastes. He especially loved

ECLECTIC:
wide-ranging, from lots of different genres.

rock and roll and soul music, and his favourite artists were Elvis Presley, Jimi Hendrix and Aretha Franklin.

Farrokh learned to play the piano and joined the school choir. He even formed a **band**, The Hectics, with some of his friends at school.

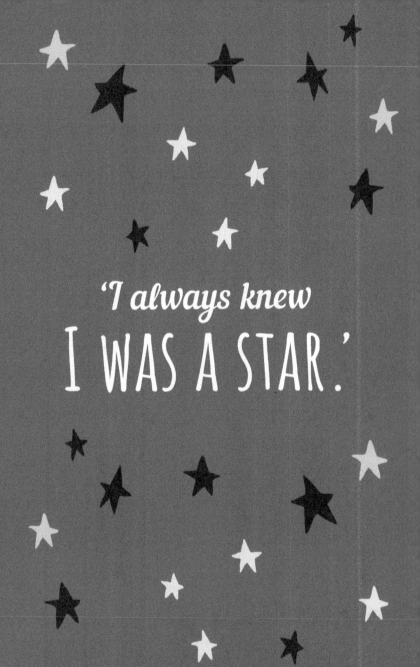

'I always knew
I WAS A STAR.'

In 1964, when Farrokh was seventeen, a revolution took place in Zanzibar. Worried about their young family, Farrokh's parents decided to flee to London.

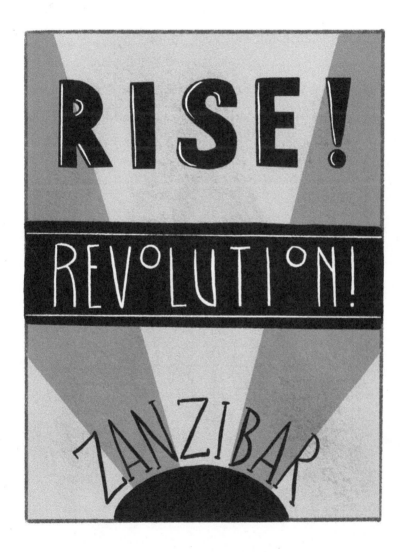

Farrokh liked living in London. He studied art at Ealing Art College, and was always going to see bands perform at pubs and bars around the city. He joined a band, and became known for his *flamboyant* fashion, incredible stage presence and wide vocal range.

When he was in his twenties Farrokh changed his name to Freddie Mercury and became the lead singer of the band Queen.

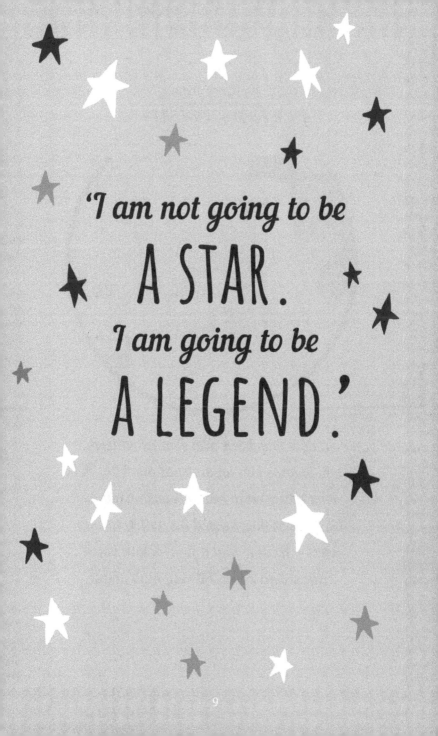

'I am not going to be

A STAR.

I am going to be

A LEGEND.'

DID YOU KNOW?

Freddie was born with four extra teeth,
which gave him an unusual overbite. He
was reluctant to have his teeth fixed as
he thought they helped his ability to sing
well - Freddie had a four-octave vocal
range and could hit very high notes.

With **Brian May** on guitar, **Roger Taylor** on drums and **John Deacon** on bass, Queen went on to have huge musical hits throughout the 1970s, 80s and 90s.

Queen are perhaps best known for their song 'Bohemian Rhapsody', a six-minute epic that has gone to number one in the UK – twice!

Top tunes

Queen's bestselling singles in the UK

'BOHEMIAN RHAPSODY' (1975)

'WE ARE THE CHAMPIONS' (1977)

'UNDER PRESSURE' - WITH DAVID BOWIE (1981)

'DON'T STOP ME NOW' (1979)

'CRAZY LITTLE THING CALLED LOVE' (1979)

'RADIO GAGA' (1984)

'I WANT TO BREAK FREE' (1984)

'SOMEBODY TO LOVE' (1976)

'KILLER QUEEN' (1974)

'A KIND OF MAGIC' (1986)

The band became known for their **extravagant** live shows, inspired by Freddie's love of ballet, theatre and opera.

As well as his amazing voice and stage presence, Freddie was a talented songwriter – he wrote ten of the seventeen songs on Queen's *Greatest Hits* album, including 'Bohemian Rhapsody' and 'Killer Queen'.

When he was in his thirties Freddie was diagnosed with HIV, a virus that attacks the *immune system* and makes it harder for someone to fight off infections. Freddie died of bronchial pneumonia caused by AIDS (acquired immune deficiency syndrome) on 24 November 1991. He continues to be remembered as one of the greatest musicians and songwriters in the world.

This is his extraordinary life.

'The most important
thing, darling,
IS TO LIVE A
FABULOUS LIFE.
As long as it's fabulous,
I DON'T CARE
HOW LONG IT IS.'

Growing up

*F*arrokh was the name given to Freddie at birth by his parents, Bomi and Jer. Farrokh's father, Bomi, was from a poor family who lived in Gujarat, India, and because there was little work to be found there he moved to *Zanzibar* in Tanzania.

Once there, Bomi worked for the British government, and *travelled* all over Tanzania as part of his job. Despite his humble upbringing, Bomi amassed a *small fortune*, and was able to live very comfortably. He had his own house and a car, which was unusual for the time. Bomi longed for a family, and someone to share his money with.

During a trip to India to visit his family, Bomi met **Jer**. They fell in love and were married. Soon afterwards Jer left her family and her life in India behind to live with her new husband in Zanzibar. In 1946 Jer gave birth to their first child, their son Farrokh.

From a young age Farrokh showed a *passion for music*. He enjoyed a wide range of genres, including folk, classical and Indian music. Known for being funny and CHARISMATIC, he would accompany his parents to functions and parties, and was always delighted when he was asked to sing for the guests.

CHARISMATIC: outgoing and charming.

When Farrokh was six his little sister **Kashmira** was born. Farrokh loved her very much, and was extremely proud and *protective* of her.

Life at school

At eight Farrokh was sent to St Peter's, an English boarding school in India.

Farrokh was shy at first. He had been born with four extra teeth and his classmates teased him and called him 'Bucky'. He was very *self-conscious* about his teeth, and would cover them up with his top lip, or cover his mouth with his hands when he was laughing.

Later in life, Freddie would say that his unusual teeth gave him his unique singing voice and wide vocal range.

While he was at St Peter's Farrokh's teachers gave him the nickname 'Freddie'. He liked the name so much that he decided to keep it, and soon became known as Freddie Bulsara.

Freddie was good at art and sports. He once won a trophy for 'Best All-rounder' – he was so proud that he wrote a letter home to his mum and dad:

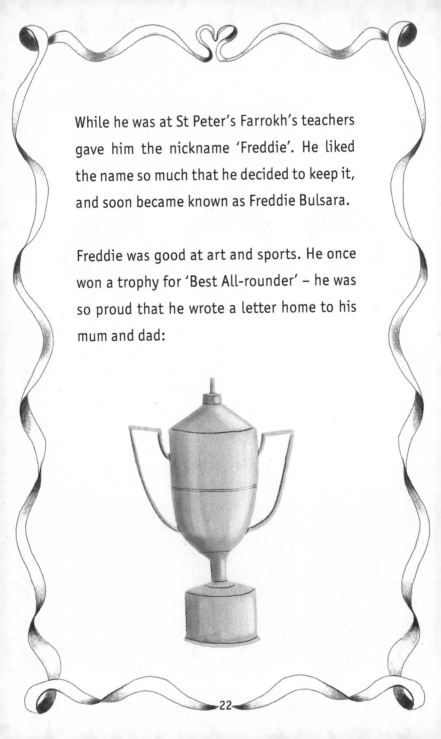

Dear Mum and Dad,

I hope you are all well and Kashmira's cold is better.

Don't worry, I'm fine. Me and my friends at the Ashleigh House are like a second family. The teachers are very strict and discipline is most important here at St Peter's.

I'm very happy to tell you that I was awarded the big trophy, Best All-rounder. I received a big trophy and they even took a photograph, which will appear in the annual school magazine. I'm very proud and I hope you are too.

Send my love to Kash. I love my little sister as I love you all.

Farrokh

He joined the school choir and took piano lessons. He became known for being able to *play by ear*; he could listen to a song on the radio and was immediately able to play it himself on the piano.

Freddie formed his first band, The Hectics, with his friends Bruce Murray, Farang Irani, Derrick Branche

and Victory Rana. The boys were all fans of **Elvis Presley** and would play covers of American rock and roll songs like 'Tutti Frutti' by Little Richard, 'Yakkety Yak' by The Coasters and 'Whole Lotta Lovin'' by Fats Domino. They would dress like American rock and roll stars in white shirts, black ties and pleated trousers, their hair slicked back with grease.

Despite Freddie's impressive vocal range, Bruce was the lead singer, while Freddie played boogie-woogie piano and provided **backing vocals**.

Although he was good at sport, art and music, Freddie didn't do as well in other subjects at school. Towards the end of his time at St Peter's, Freddie had become **so focused** on The Hectics and his music that his other grades began to slip. When he was fifteen he **failed** his end-of-year exams, and he left school before he could complete his O levels (a GCSE equivalent).

Life in Zanzibar

Since 1890 Zanzibar had been a PROTECTORATE of the British Empire, which means Britain partly controlled the country. In 1963, when the protectorate was ended, Zanzibar became a monarchy led by Sultan Jamshid bin Abdullah. However, tensions grew between the two major political parties: the Zanzibar Nationalist Party, which was made up mostly of Arabs and Indians, and the Afro-Shirazi Party, which was made up mostly of Africans.

PROTECTORATE:
a country
that is controlled
by another.

In 1964 the Sultan was DEPOSED during what has come to be known as the Zanzibar Revolution. Many Arabs and Indians were killed.

DEPOSED:
removed from a position of power suddenly and forcefully.

Bomi and Jer decided to flee the country. Since they had both been born in India, Bomi and Jer considered moving back there. But as Bomi had worked for the British government he had a **British passport** and decided to take his family to England.

Stuffing whatever they could carry into two suitcases, Bomi, Jer, Freddie and Kashmira flew to England, where they settled into a **four-bedroom house** at 22 Gladstone Avenue, Feltham, London. Freddie was seventeen years old.

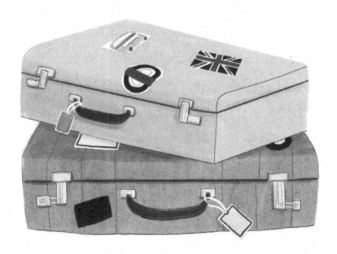

London

$\mathcal{A}$fter settling in London, Bomi worked as an accountant for a local catering company, and Jer worked for Marks & Spencer.

Freddie – who had always had a fondness for Western culture, especially rock and roll and fashion – **thrived** in the big city. He spent his time going to gigs at pubs and colleges, sleeping on friends' floors when he missed the train back home. What little money he had went on **clothes and records**. He became known for his **flamboyant** fashion, which included skinny drainpipe trousers that were too small and slicked-back hair.

Though he had struggled at school in India, Freddie became focused on getting into **art college**. He was a talented artist, and he also knew that many of his musical idols had gone to art college too.

Soon after arriving in London Freddie attended Isleworth Polytechnic, where he took the course he needed in order to get into art college. He went on to study **Graphic Art and Design** at Ealing Art College.

Jimi Hendrix

Freddie was a big fan of the American guitarist *Jimi Hendrix*. He first saw Jimi perform his song 'Hey Joe' on the television programme *Ready Steady Go!* Freddie was so **captivated** by Jimi's performance that he went to see him play live fourteen times – including nine nights in a row at pubs and bars all over London. Freddie even drew pictures of Jimi that he used to decorate his bedroom walls.

Jimi, who was only four years older than Freddie, was a huge inspiration. Freddie soon began to crave the stage.

Bands

While he was at college Freddie joined a number of bands, such as Ibex (later called Wreckage) and Sour Milk Sea.

While he was performing with Ibex one night, Freddie developed what would become one of his signature moves. When Freddie picked up the **micro-phone stand** to move it out of the way, the stand broke in half. Freddie was left holding the top half.

Instead of removing the microphone, Freddie held on to the stand, using it to dance with and strike a pose onstage. Throughout his career he would appear with the top half of a microphone stand – including at his iconic performance at *Live Aid* in 1985.

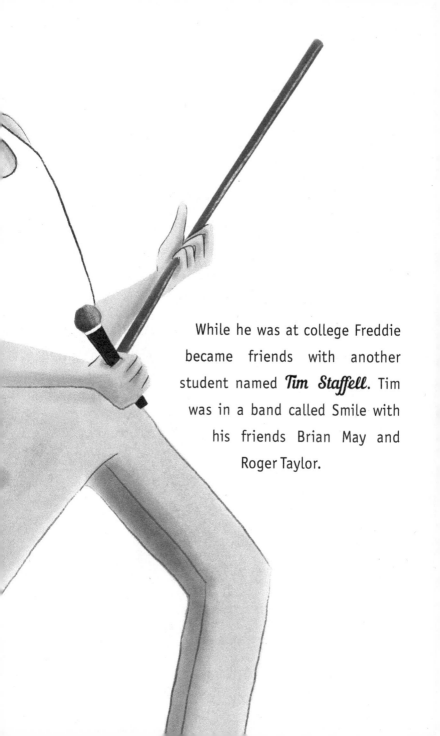

While he was at college Freddie became friends with another student named *Tim Staffell*. Tim was in a band called Smile with his friends Brian May and Roger Taylor.

Falling in love

When Freddie lived in London he met Mary Austin, who was a friend of Brian May. Mary worked in a shop called Biba, which became known for selling outrageous clothes and being a popular hang-out for rock stars and celebrities. Freddie – who was already known for his flamboyant fashion – was a frequent customer.

One day, he plucked up the courage to ask Mary out on a date. Freddie and Mary fell in love, and they soon started living together.

Freddie sold ***second-hand clothes*** at a stall on Kensington Market, and worked as a baggage handler at Heathrow Airport. Neither Mary nor Freddie made very much money. The couple were so poor they could only afford one pair of curtains.

Brian May was born in Hampton, Middlesex. He was brilliant at science and graduated from Hampton Grammar School with four A levels in physics, mathematics, applied mathematics and additional mathematics. When Freddie and Brian met, Brian was a student at Imperial College London, where he studied physics and maths. Later in life Brian would go on to achieve a PhD, the highest possible university degree, in **astrophysics**.

DID YOU KNOW?

Brian plays a guitar he built with the help of his dad, Harold, when he was sixteen. The neck of the guitar is made from a piece of wood taken from the family fireplace! Brian's guitar is nicknamed 'The Red Special'.

Roger Taylor was born in King's Lynn, Norfolk. Originally Roger had learned to play the ukulele and the guitar. However, inspired by Keith Moon of The Who, he started playing the drums, and became known for his unique sound and playing style. When Freddie and Roger met, Roger was studying to be a ***dentist***!

Queen

*F*reddie was a big fan of Smile and would follow the band around to gigs, sometimes riding with them in their van. Later Tim left Smile to join another band, and Freddie took his place as lead singer. It was Freddie's idea to change the band's name to Queen.

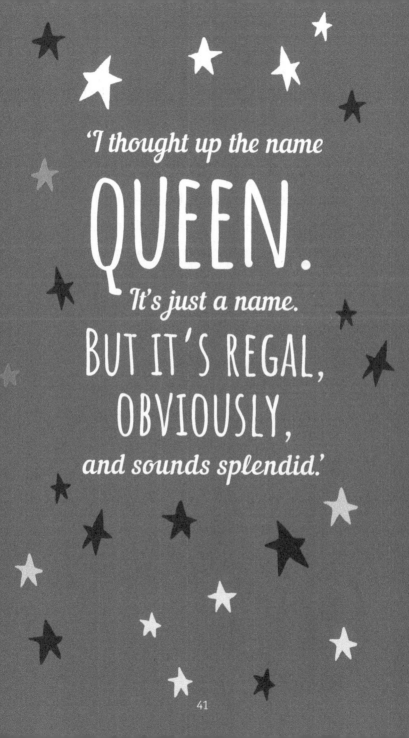

'I thought up the name

QUEEN.

It's just a name.

BUT IT'S REGAL,
OBVIOUSLY,

and sounds splendid.'

Knowing they needed to bulk out their sound, the band began to audition for a bass player. After several unsuccessful auditions, they met *John Deacon*.

John Deacon was born in Leicester. His friends nicknamed him 'Deaks' or 'Deaky', nicknames that stuck throughout his time in the band. When Freddie and John met, John was studying electronics at Chelsea College in London. John had already seen Queen perform the year before – and he wasn't that impressed! However, after Queen lost their original bassist, John decided to join the band.

With all the band members in place Queen began to tour colleges, pubs and venues around London and the rest of the country.

Freddie designed Queen's logo. Resembling a coat of arms, the logo incorporates the zodiac signs of each band member – two lions representing Roger and John, who are both Leos; a crab representing Brian, who is a Cancer; and two fairies for Freddie, whose star sign was Virgo. The symbols surround a large letter Q. The Queen crest first appeared on the cover of Queen's debut album.

Queen wrote songs together, which they would play on tour. After writing a song called 'My Fairy King', featuring a line about 'Mother Mercury', Freddie decided to change his name to *Freddie Mercury*.

The band went into a recording studio to record a demo that helped them secure their first record deal. Soon it was time to make an album.

'IF I DIDN'T DO THIS

I wouldn't have anything to do.'

1973
TOP HIT
'KEEP YOURSELF
ALIVE'
QUEEN

Queen's sound

Queen's first few albums were recorded at Trident, a recording studio in London that was very popular at the time. Queen were allowed to use the studio for free, but had to wait until the paying bands had finished, so most of their songs were recorded late at night and into the early hours of the morning!

The band were known for being **perfectionists**.

1974
TOP HIT
'SEVEN SEAS OF RHYE'
QUEEN II

1974
TOP HIT
'KILLER QUEEN'
SHEER HEART ATTACK

'WE'RE SEEKING PERFECTION, *even if we know it's virtually impossible to find* . . . WE ARE METICULOUS. *It drives some promoters and backstage staff guys mad,* BUT WE WANT EVERYTHING TO BE *as good as it can* FOR OUR AUDIENCES.'

Queen's sound was so perfect that it was rumoured some of the guitar and vocal sounds were synthesizers, which led to the band including the line

'AND NO ONE PLAYED SYNTHESIZERS'

on all of their album covers!

SYNTHESIZER:
a sound created using keyboards and computers.

The albums *Queen* and *Queen II* featured the band's unique sound, a blend of heavy metal and classic rock, with songs about ogres, queens and giant rats. Brian May would play huge **guitar riffs**, and the songs were complemented by Roger Taylor's high-pitched **vocal harmonies**. But it was Freddie's incredible voice that set them apart from the rest – he could sing songs in a low baritone or a high tenor, and had a four-octave range, which is unusual for a man.

By the time they came to record their third album, *Sheer Heart Attack*, the band had become more experimental, amping up their harmonies and approaching their lyrics with the same **camp sense of humour** that Freddie was known for. One of the stand-out songs on the album was 'Killer Queen', featuring four-part harmonies, a multi-layered guitar solo by Brian May and two basslines from John Deacon. The song won Freddie his first Ivor Novello Award for songwriting.

'"KILLER QUEEN"
I wrote in one night.
I'M NOT BEING
CONCEITED
OR ANYTHING,
*but it just fell
into place.'*

When it was released as a single 'Killer Queen' was the band's biggest hit to date – but it was nothing compared to what was to come.

'Bohemian Rhapsody'

Freddie began writing the song 'Bohemian Rhapsody' when he was a student at Ealing Art College in 1968. There he came up with the song's opening line: *'Mama, just killed a man.'* By 1975 the song had become a six-minute epic!

1975
TOP HITS
'BOHEMIAN RHAPSODY',
'YOU'RE MY BEST FRIEND'
A NIGHT AT
THE OPERA

DID YOU KNOW?

The word 'Bohemian' refers to a group of artists who lived in the 1800s. They were known for defying convention – a bit like Freddie himself! A rhapsody is a piece of classical music without a rigid structure, but that tends to be very emotional in character.

The song was *split into three parts*: the opening ballad; the operatic middle section; and the heavy hard-rock ending, complete with Brian May's iconic guitar solo. It took over three weeks and five different recording studios to record this one song. (Most bands take three weeks to record a whole album!)

When Freddie first played 'Bohemian Rhapsody' for Roy Thomas Baker, who produced Queen's *A Night at the Opera* album, he stopped after the opening section of the song. Freddie turned to Roy and said, 'This is when the *operatic section* comes in.' Roy laughed, thinking Freddie was joking. Roy was shocked when Freddie turned up at the recording studio with huge wads of paper – including an old phone book, Post-its and notes from his dad's work – with the whole operatic section written out, determined to make it a reality!

The harmonies on the operatic section of the song are all sung by members of Queen, with Brian May taking the lower end of the range, Roger Taylor the higher end and Freddie the middle.

The band recorded over 180 parts for the song to make up the sound of a powerful operatic choir. They would later say in interviews that the tape they had used to record the song on became **transparent** because it had been recorded over so many times.

With the recording complete Queen wanted to **release the song as a single**, but their management and record company thought it was too strange, and that no one would play a six-minute song on the radio.

DID YOU KNOW?

Even Freddie's friend Elton John told him the song was 'too weird' to release.

In a bid to prove them wrong Freddie took a copy of the record with him when he went to visit his friend Kenny Everett. Kenny was a comedian and DJ who presented a breakfast show on the Capital FM radio station.

Kenny teased the audience, saying he had a song he wasn't allowed to play, and then playing snippets from 'Bohemian Rhapsody' over the course of his show, before finally playing the whole song. He went on to play it fourteen times over two days.

The radio station was INUNDATED with phone calls from fans wanting to know where they could buy the record – even though it hadn't been released!

INUNDATED: overwhelmed, flooded.

The operatic section features references to lots of obscure, unusual characters. **Scaramouche** is a clown from sixteenth-century Italian theatre; **Galileo** refers to the sixteenth-century Italian astronomer; **Figaro** is a clever character from the opera *The Barber of Seville*; and **Beelzebub** is one of the many names given to the Devil. The section also features the Arabic word *Bismillah*, after a phrase in the Qur'an: *'Bismi-llahi r-rahmani r-rahiim'*, which means 'In the name of Allah, the Most Gracious, the Most Merciful'.

The iconic video

*A*s 'Bohemian Rhapsody' stormed up the charts, the band hit another snag – the song was too complicated to perform live on television.

With a performance on the television show *Top of the Pops* looming, Queen went into a **rehearsal studio** to record their first **music video**. It took four hours and cost £3,500 to make – and it was money well spent, as fans liked the video so much that *Top of the Pops* kept playing it, keeping the song at the top of the charts.

The video used special effects that were very futuristic at the time. To create the effect of multiple images of the band members during the operatic section, the director placed a **prism** on the camera lens.

Queen had taken a huge risk with 'Bohemian Rhapsody' and their album *A Night at the Opera*. The recording had taken three long months and cost the band £35,000 – the most expensive album ever made at the time – but the risk paid off. 'Bohemian Rhapsody' was Queen's first ***number-one single***, selling over a million copies in the UK and topping the charts in the UK, Australia, Canada, the Netherlands, New Zealand and Belgium. 1975's *A Night at the Opera* was their first number-one album.

DID YOU KNOW?

Following the success of 'Bohemian Rhapsody', drummer Roger Taylor had to add a huge gong to his drum kit to provide the final note of the song. The gong had to be cleaned every night, and took ages to set up and take down.

Controversial videos

Queen were famous for their funny, sometimes CONTROVERSIAL, videos.

The video for 'I Want to Break Free' from Queen's album *The Works* is a popular one, featuring all the members of Queen dressed as women. The video is based on the soap opera *Coronation Street*. Freddie appears as a **bored housewife** hoovering the carpet.

CONTROVERSIAL: much discussed; provoking a strong reaction.

He is dressed in a skirt and heels, with a huge beehive hairdo, but kept his signature moustache.

The video was controversial for depicting the singers dressed as women – some people believe it is one of the reasons Queen started to become less popular in America.

Freddie and fame

*F*reddie began to enjoy his new fame, spending his fortune on Japanese art and partying.

He became known for hosting **huge lavish parties** at his home in London or in nightclubs around the world. Freddie would fly his friends in from all over the world, paying for expensive hotels and flights on the supersonic jet Concorde, which was the fastest passenger plane at the time. Freddie would turn up in **elaborate costumes**, such as sequinned catsuits and army jackets with enormous shoulder pads.

DID YOU KNOW?

Lady Gaga is such a big Freddie fan that she named herself after Queen's hit song 'Radio Ga Ga'.

'I've worked hard
for money . . .
I'VE EARNED IT
SO IT'S MINE
to do what
I want with.'

Freddie's birthday parties were especially legendary! One year he gave a party for 500 of his friends at Xenon, a nightclub in London. Freddie's birthday cake was *1.5 metres long* and decorated to look like a Rolls-Royce.

For his thirty-ninth birthday he threw a **Black and White Drag Ball** at a nightclub in Munich. Guests were required to wear black and white and come dressed as the opposite gender. Guests included some of the most famous pop stars of the day, including Phil Collins, Diana Ross and Little Richard, as well as the famous drag queen Divine.

Freddie once went clubbing with his friend the DJ and comedian Kenny Everett and *Princess Diana*! Knowing the famous princess would probably draw attention, Freddie persuaded her to disguise herself as a man, and took her out to a London gay bar in an army jacket and sunglasses.

'I really need
DANGER
and
EXCITEMENT.
I'm never scared of
PUTTING MYSELF
OUT ON A LIMB.'

Although he was known for being a *party animal*, Freddie was actually quite shy, and would sometimes talk about *feeling lonely*.

'Success has brought me
WORLD IDOLIZATION
AND MILLIONS OF POUNDS.
But it has prevented me
from having
THE ONE THING WE ALL NEED,
A LOVING,
ON-GOING RELATIONSHIP.'

Freddie adopted an old theatrical custom
of calling men by women's names. He
nicknamed his friend Elton John 'Sharon
Cavendish', and Freddie himself became
'Melina', after the Greek actress Melina
Mercouri. Brian May was nicknamed
Maggie, after Rod Stewart's hit song 'Maggie
May', and Roger Taylor was nicknamed Liz,
after the actress Elizabeth Taylor. Freddie
reversed the tradition with Mary Austin,
who he nicknamed Steve, after Steve Austin,
the main character from the TV show
The Six Million Dollar Man.

Coming out

*F*reddie had relationships with both women and men throughout his life.

In 1976 Freddie **came out** to his girlfriend, Mary Austin, about whom he had written the song 'Love of My Life', and to whom he had proposed in 1973. He confessed that he had secretly been having relationships with men and told her he was bisexual. Freddie and Mary split up, though they remained close friends throughout his life.

1976
TOP HITS
'SOMEBODY TO LOVE',
'TIE YOUR MOTHER
DOWN'
A DAY AT THE RACES

'All my lovers asked me why they COULDN'T REPLACE MARY, but it's simply IMPOSSIBLE. The only friend I've got is Mary, AND I DON'T WANT ANYBODY ELSE.'

Celebrate Bisexuality Day

In 1999 some LGBTQ+ activists were fed up with the fact that people didn't seem to know much about bisexual people. They came up with the idea of Celebrate Bisexuality Day to help raise understanding and awareness. They decided that this day would take place in September as a tribute to Freddie. Celebrate Bisexuality Day now takes place on 23 September, and the week surrounding it is Bisexual+ Awareness Week.

LGBTQ+:
a term for someone who identifies as lesbian, gay, bisexual, transgender, queer or many other terms denoted by '+'.

Freddie and cats

While Freddie and Mary Austin were living together they adopted two cats, Tom and Jerry, and it was the beginning of a lifelong love affair for Freddie!

Freddie treated his cats like they were his children. He would *spoil* them with toys and treats, and even made sure they each had a little stocking with presents to open at Christmas. He would phone to speak to them while he was away on tour, having his assistants hold the phone up to his cats. Freddie adopted most of his cats from *rescue centres* and would eventually have ten cats at his home in London, Garden Lodge.

Freddie even dedicated his solo album *Mr Bad Guy* to his cat.

'This album is dedicated to MY CAT JERRY – ALSO TOM, OSCAR AND TIFFANY, AND ALL THE CAT LOVERS *across the universe!'*

Freddie's favourite cat was Delilah, a tabby cat he adopted in 1987. He loved Delilah so much that he even recorded a song about her. 'Delilah' starts off sounding like Freddie is singing to a woman – 'Delilah, oh my, oh

my, oh my, you're irresistible' – until he gets to the line about Delilah 'peeing all over my Chippendale Suite'!

In the last video Freddie made with Queen, Freddie wore his favourite waistcoat, which was decorated with pictures of his cats.

After recording their album *Hot Space*, Queen were tired from a ***relentless touring schedule***. The band had begun to bicker and argue, so they took a break.

Brian May left to collaborate with Eddie Van Halen, and Freddie went off to work on his own solo album, *Mr Bad Guy*. Unlike Queen, who were known for their rock sound, Freddie's solo songs drew on his love of ***disco and dance music***.

1977
TOP HITS
'WE ARE THE CHAMPIONS',
'WE WILL ROCK YOU'
NEWS OF THE WORLD

1978
TOP HITS
'BICYCLE RACE', 'FAT BOTTOMED GIRLS', 'DON'T STOP ME NOW'
JAZZ

1980
TOP HIT
'FLASH'S THEME'
FLASH GORDON

1982
TOP HIT
'UNDER PRESSURE' –
WITH DAVID BOWIE
HOT SPACE

1980
TOP HITS
'ANOTHER ONE BITES THE DUST',
'CRAZY LITTLE THING
CALLED LOVE'
THE GAME

Recording the album was very taxing, as Freddie wrote and performed all the songs himself, and also oversaw the production and sound engineering. Freddie recorded some songs for the album with **Michael Jackson**, but the two of them didn't get along very well.

Freddie would go on to record another album without Queen, called *Barcelona*, with the famous opera singer Montserrat Caballé.

DID YOU KNOW?

Although *Mr Bad Guy* was his first solo album, Freddie had released music on his own before. In 1973, before Queen's first album was released, Freddie recorded the songs 'I Can Hear Music' and 'Goin' Back' with the producer Robin Geoffrey Cable – the songs were released under the stage name Larry Lurex.

1984
TOP HITS
'RADIO GA GA',
'I WANT TO BREAK FREE',
'HAMMER
TO FALL'
THE WORKS

Live Aid

*I*n 1985 rock stars Bob Geldof and Midge Ure put together a huge charity rock concert called **Live Aid**.

The concert took place in two locations at once – Wembley Stadium in London, and John F. Kennedy Stadium in Philadelphia in the USA – and was **broadcast live** on television and radio around the world. The aim of the concert was to raise money for people in Ethiopia, who were experiencing a famine.

Some of the biggest bands and musicians of the 1980s –
including Elton John, George Michael, Madonna and
David Bowie – performed throughout the day and into
the night. Queen took to the stage in London just after
6 p.m. and performed a short seventeen-minute set that
included some of their best-known hits:

'Bohemian Rhapsody'
'Radio Ga Ga'
'Hammer to Fall'
'Crazy Little Thing Called Love'
'We Will Rock You'
'We Are the Champions'

In the middle of the concert Freddie took to the centre of the stage to **_have fun with the crowd_**. Without any backing music Freddie sang a musical phrase – sometimes one note, sometimes a vocal run – and the crowd would repeat it back to him. Clearly enjoying himself, Freddie sang one long extended note at the end, which became known as 'The Note Heard Around the World'. The performance was not only the highlight of the day for many people, but went on to be regarded as one of the **_best live performances_** in the history of rock. The concert raised over £150 million.

1986
TOP HITS
'ONE VISION', 'A KIND OF MAGIC', 'WHO WANTS TO LIVE FOREVER'
A KIND OF MAGIC

In love again

$\mathcal{D}$uring this time Freddie met a man called Jim Hutton.

Freddie went to gay clubs all around the world, including the **Copacabana** in London. Here Freddie met Jim, an Irish hairdresser. Freddie and Jim hit it off and began to meet regularly over the next two years. They soon became a couple, and Freddie lived with Jim for the rest of his life.

Illness and death

*I*n 1987 Freddie was diagnosed as HIV-positive.

HIV stands for Human Immunodeficiency Virus. It is a virus that affects the immune system, your body's way of protecting you against disease. If untreated, HIV can cause the immune system to become weaker. It becomes harder to fight off infections. HIV cannot be cured the way some viruses can, so when somebody is diagnosed as HIV-positive they need to take medication to stay well. With medication a lot of people can live full happy lives with the virus. Some children are born with HIV because their mothers have it. Adults can get HIV through sexual intercourse, or if they come into contact with the blood of someone who has the virus.

Nowadays it's possible for people with HIV to live a long, healthy life. Medicines have been developed that stop the virus from making more copies of itself inside the body, meaning that almost everyone who takes this medication can't pass the virus on to anyone else.

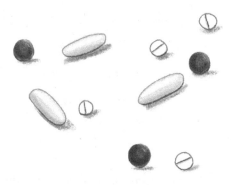

However, when Freddie was diagnosed with HIV very little was known about the virus. Treatment was much less advanced at that time, and many HIV-positive people were unable to get successful medication. As a result these people were at risk of AIDS, a collection of life-threatening health problems caused by the untreated virus severely weakening the immune system.

AIDS: stands for Acquired Immune Deficiency Syndome.

The **lack of knowledge and understanding** about HIV at the time made a lot of the general public feel worried, and often unfair judgements were made about people who were HIV-positive. This may have been why Freddie chose to keep his diagnosis secret and tell only a few people about it.

HIV had made Freddie very ill. Photos of him appearing thin and frail had led the press to **speculate** about his illness, although he continued to keep it a secret from everyone but his closest friends.

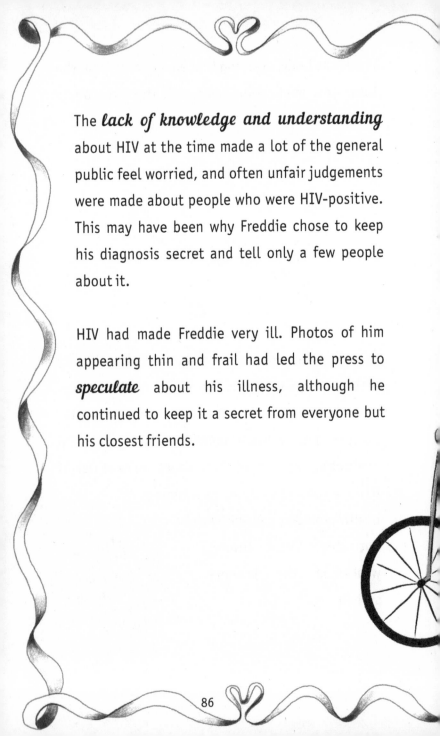

In 1990 Queen went back into the studio to record their album *Innuendo*. The album features 'These Are the Days of Our Lives', which was released as a single. Queen's manager had an animated video made for the song in case Freddie would be too ill to appear in a video himself. But Freddie was determined. The video was filmed in black-and-white to disguise how frail Freddie had become. A lesion on his foot meant he was in incredible pain on the set of the video and had to remain standing in one place for most of his performance.

1989
TOP HIT
'I WANT IT ALL'
THE MIRACLE

1991
TOP HITS
'THE SHOW MUST GO ON',
'THESE ARE THE DAYS OF
OUR LIVES'
INNUENDO

At the end of the video Freddie looks into the camera and whispers the line

'I still love you.'

Many people have taken this to be Freddie's way of saying goodbye to his fans. This was his final performance.

His last months

By 1991 the drugs Freddie was taking to manage his illness had stopped working, so Freddie decided not to take them. There were no more treatments available.

Knowing that
he didn't have much time
left, Freddie retired to Garden Lodge,
his home in Kensington, where he would live
out what was left of his life.

By now Freddie was struggling to walk and used a cane to get around. His speech was slower, and his eyesight was failing. He spent most of his time in bed watching television and films.

He was cared for by his boyfriend, Jim, his former girlfriend Mary, his chef, Joe Fanelli, his assistant, Peter Freestone, and his friend Dave Clark. He remained close with his family, including his sister, throughout his life, and they visited him while he was unwell. He also had visits from his friends, including his bandmates and the singer Elton John.

The press continued to speculate about Freddie having AIDS. Sometimes as many as seventy reporters would gather outside his house. To make sure that none of the newspapers got the scoop on his illness, Freddie and his team prepared a *statement*, which they released to the newspapers on 23 November 1991:

Following the enormous conjecture in the press over the last two weeks, I wish to confirm that I have been tested HIV-positive and have AIDS. I felt it correct to keep this information private to date to protect the privacy of those around me.

However, the time has come now for my friends and fans around the world to know the truth and I hope that everyone will join with my doctors and all those worldwide in the fight against this terrible disease.

My privacy has always been very special to me and I am famous for my lack of interviews. Please understand this policy will continue.

Freddie died a day later.

Tribute concert for AIDS awareness

*F*ollowing Freddie's death, Queen rereleased 'Bohemian Rhapsody', with all the proceeds from the sales of the record going to the Terence Higgins Trust, a charity that works to support people living with HIV. The charity also aims to **educate** people about HIV and end STIGMA. The song went straight to number one in the charts and raised over **£1 million** for the charity.

STIGMA:
a strong feeling of disapproval people associate with something, often unfairly.

On Easter Monday 1992 Queen helped put on the Freddie Mercury Tribute Concert for AIDS Awareness at Wembley Stadium. It was a huge rock and roll event, and 72,000 tickets sold out within three hours before a line-up had even been announced. The concert was broadcast live on television and radio in seventy-six different countries to an audience of one billion people.

The remaining members of Queen – John Deacon, Brian May and Roger Taylor – were joined onstage by stars like David Bowie, Elton John, Annie Lennox and George Michael to sing some of Queen's *biggest hit songs*.

Video footage of Freddie and his performances was played throughout.

The concert was later voted the greatest live rock event of the 1990s and proceeds from the concert helped launch the Mercury Phoenix Trust, an AIDS charity.

During his childhood Freddie was an avid stamp collector, so he would have been delighted by the special stamp issued by the Royal Mail in 1999 that celebrated his life. The photograph on the stamp shows Freddie onstage with his signature microphone stand. In the background you can see the silhouette of Roger Taylor playing the drums. Roger Taylor's presence, however, caused some controversy – until 2005 the only living people allowed to appear on British stamps were members of the British royal family. No doubt Freddie would have enjoyed the controversy!

Made in Heaven

In 1995, four years after Freddie died, Queen released their fifteenth and final studio album, *Made in Heaven*. Freddie's vocals were taken from previously unreleased songs, as well as songs he had written and recorded during the last years of his life.

1995
TOP HIT
'HEAVEN FOR EVERYONE'
MADE IN HEAVEN

'A Winter's Tale' was the last song Freddie wrote himself. Unlike most of Queen's songs, because Freddie was so unwell, it was recorded in **one take.**

The song 'Mother Love', written by Freddie and Brian May, was the last song Freddie recorded.

The album went straight to number one in the UK and has now sold around twenty million copies around the world. The cover of the album features a statue of Freddie created by Czech sculptor Irena Sedlecká. The statue now stands at Lake Geneva in Montreal, Switzerland, where Queen recorded most of their albums, and where Freddie lived for much of his later life.

Queen today

*F*ollowing Freddie's death, John Deacon retired from music. But Brian May and Roger Taylor **continue to perform** as Queen. They helped close the Olympics in London in 2012, performing with Jessie J, who entered the arena wearing a yellow jacket with a huge train, designed to resemble one that Freddie had worn.

Freddie was present via a specially animated video of him performing vocal runs, which was taken from a concert Queen performed at Wembley Stadium in 1986. As they did then, the Olympic crowd repeated the vocal runs back to him.

In 1990, Queen were awarded a **Brit Award** for their Outstanding Contribution to British Music.

Queen now perform with the singer **Adam Lambert** and continue to tour sold-out stadiums around the world.

Queen's music remains popular around the world, and Freddie is always **_winning over_** new fans.

In life, Freddie went from Farrokh Bulsara, a shy little boy who dropped out of school before sitting his exams, to Freddie Mercury, the flamboyant frontman of one of the world's best-known and most-loved bands, with a spectacular singing voice, a serious talent for song-writing and a **_legendary_** stage presence.

Freddie's brave decision to come out about having AIDS made him one of the most prominent public figures to talk openly about being affected by the virus. Freddie helped bring public attention to the AIDS crisis at a time when people weren't comfortable talking about it.

He will always be remembered as a star and a legend.

TIMELINE

1946

Freddie Mercury is born
Farrokh Bulsara in Stone Town,
Zanzibar, in Tanzania, Africa.

1954

Freddie goes to St
Peter's, an English
boarding school in India.

1958

Freddie forms The Hectics with
some of his school friends and
starts using the name Freddie.

1970

Freddie joins Smile with
Brian May and Roger Taylor,
renaming the band Queen.

1969

Freddie meets Mary Austin,
just after finishing art
college. They soon become
a couple.

1966

Freddie starts studying
Graphic Art and Design at
Ealing Art College.

1964

Following the Zanzibar Revolution,
Freddie and his family move to
Middlesex, England.

1971

John Deacon joins Queen.

1973

Queen release their first album, *Queen*.

1975

'Bohemian Rhapsody' is released – it reaches number one in the charts and stays there for nine weeks.

Queen's album *A Night at the Opera* is released – it goes straight to number one in the charts.

1976

Freddie's romantic relationship with Mary Austin ends, though they remain friends throughout his life.

1991

The album *Innuendo* is released.

The day before he dies Freddie announces that he has AIDS.

Freddie dies of bronchial pneumonia aged forty-five.

1990

Queen receive a Brit Award for their Outstanding Contribution to British Music.

1987

Freddie Mercury is diagnosed as HIV-positive. The diagnosis is kept secret from the public.

1985

Freddie releases his first solo album, *Mr Bad Guy*.

Freddie's legendary performance at Live Aid.

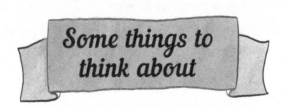

Some things to think about

Freddie went from working a stall on Kensington Market selling second-hand clothes, with very little money, to being a world-famous rock star. He followed his dreams and proved if you work hard enough you can achieve your goals.

What are your dreams for your future?

Is there anything holding you back from achieving them?

Queen were, and still are, an internationally recognized household name.

What do you think it was about Queen that made them so popular, even today?

Some things to think about

Since the 1980s LGBTQ+ rights, and conversations about AIDS and HIV, have come much further.

What work do you think still needs to be done to create equality for all?

Freddie acknowledged that at the height of his fame, despite being successful and having lots of money, he was still lonely.

Why do you think this is?

Is it really true that money can't bring you happiness?

Index

Quote Sources

Direct quotes throughout are taken from
http://www.freddiemercury.com/en/quotes_by_Freddie
except the following:

Page 6, 41: http://queenarchives.com/

Page 15: https://www.morrisonhotelgallery.com/collections/
iLGSdH/Bohemian-Rhapsody---Celebrating-Freddie-Mercury--
Queen-

Pages 52, 23: Matt Richards, *Somebody to Love: The Life,
Death and Legacy of Freddie Mercury* (Blink Publishing, 2017)

Page 73: Lesley-Ann Jones, M*ercury: An Intimate Biography
of Freddie Mercury* (Simon and Schuster, 2012)

Page 76: http://www.queenvault.com/

Page 99: 'Queen star dies after Aids statement'
(Guardian, 25 November 1991)

Page 115: Freddie Mercury, *A Life, In His Own Words*,
(Mercury Songs, 2006)

Illustration references

Page 43: Illustration references the Queen logo,
Freddie Mercury (1973)

Page 58: Illustration references the single cover from
'Bohemian Rhapsody', by Queen (Queen Productions, 2015)

Pages 60–61: Illustration references a still from 'I Want to
Break Free' music video, directed by David Mallett
(Limehouse Studios, 1984).

Have you read about all of these extraordinary people?